THE BOOK OF FAILURE

AARAV KAKRIA

ISBN 979-888521647-0

Contents

1. Chapter1:what Is Failure — 1

2. Chapter 2:is Failure The Next Door To Success?? — 2

3. Chapter 3:failure Is The Part Of Success — 3

4. Chapter 4: Failure — 4

5. Chapter 5: Being A Failure Is Imparitive — 5

6. Chapter6:why Failure Is The Best Teacher?? — 6

7. Why Failure Leads To Success?? — 7

ONE
CHAPTER1:WHAT IS FAILURE

WHAT IS FAILURE...........IS IT REALLY A LACK OF SUCCESS OR A STEP TO SUCCESS.FAILURE IS A THING THAT TELLS YOUR MISTAKE FROM WHICH YOU CAN IMPROVE YOUR MISTAKE.FAILURE IS A STEP FROM WHICH YOU WILL FALL HUNDREND OF TIMES BUT ONE TIME YOU WILL OPEN THE GATE OF SUCCESS.FAILURE IS THE ONLY THING WHICH EVERYONE HAS.FAILURE IS NOT THE OPPOSITE OF SUCCESS BUT A PART OF SUCCESS.FAILURE WILL MAKE YOU A PERSON WHICH YOU WANT TO BE.FAILURE IS THE ONLY THING WHICH WILL HELP YOU TO TURN A STONE INTO DIAMOND.WE SHOULD NOT GET AFRAID OF FAILURE AS IT IS THE NEXT STEP TO SUCCESS.AT THE LAST I WOULD LIKE TO SAY THAT FAILURE CREATES YOU.

TWO

CHAPTER 2:IS FAILURE THE NEXT DOOR TO SUCCESS??

ALWAYS BELIEVE IN IMPOSSIBLE" IF YOU TAKE FAILURE AS A NEGATIVE WORD THEN YOU ARE WRONG! BECAUSE THOMAS ALVA EDISON FAILED 99 TIMES TO MAKE THE BULB BUT FINALLY, HE INVENTED THE BULB AT 100th TIME.HE DID IT! HE DID NOT TAKE HIS 99 FAILS AS NEGATIVE BUT, HE LEARNT FROM HIS MISTAKES.THE SUCCESSFUL MAN WILL LEARN FROM HIS MISTAKES AND TRY AGAIN IN A DIFFERENT WAY.JUST CRYING AND WASTING YOUR TIME IS NOT THE RIGHT WAY, LEARN FROM YOUR MISTAKES AND MAKE YOUR WEAKNESS A WEAPON.IN MY OPINION "FAILURE IS THE KEY TO OPEN THE DOOR OF SUCCESS".

THREE

CHAPTER 3:FAILURE IS THE PART OF SUCCESS

"FAILURE IS THE GOLDEN KEY TO OPEN THE DOOR OF SUCCESS" WE SHOULD FAILURE AS A STEPPING STONE TO SUCCESS.IF YOU EVER GET STRESSED BECAUSE OF FAILURE JUST REMEMBER ALBERT EINSTIEN,AS HE FAILED MORE THAN 100 TIMES INVENTING E=MC2 BUT AFTER INVENTING HE THOUGHT THAT FAILURE HELPED HIM INVENTING SOMETHING. FAILURE IS NOT THE THING WHICH HURTS YOU BUT FAILURE IS THE THING WHICH IMPROVES YOU.WE SHOULD USE FAILURE AS A WEPON .FAILUREN IS A THING WHICH HELPS YOU TO TOUCH THE SKY OF SUCCESS.FAILURE AND SUCCESS ARE TWO PARALLEL WORDS NOT OPPOSITE.

FOUR
CHAPTER 4: FAILURE

FAILURE IS NOTHING IN THIS WORLD,IT IS JUST A WORD WHICH **SCARES**YOU" IF U WILL GET SCARED OF FAILURE THEN SUCCESS WILL NEVER FOLLOW YOU.IF YOU THINK THAT A PERSON WHO NEVER MAKES MISTAKE IS BETTER THAN YOU THEN YOU ARE WRONG BECAUSE A PERSON WHO NEVER MAKES MISTAKE, NEVER TRIED ANYTHING NEW. IF YOU FAIL ALWAYS SAY TO YOURSELF THAT "I HAVE NOT FAILED I JUST FOUND NEW WAYS THAT WON'T WORK.IF EVERYTHING GOES AGAINST YOU REMEMBER THAT THE AIRPLANE TAKES OFF AGAINST THE WIND,NOT WITH IT. NO ONE LIKES TO FAIL BUT FAILURE COMES IN YOUR LIFE TO MAKE YOU AN EXTRAORDINARY PERSON.LOSERS QUIT WHEN THEY FAIL , BUT WINNERS FAIL UNTIL THEY SUCCEED.

FIVE

CHAPTER 5: BEING A FAILURE IS IMPARITIVE

AS TRULY SAID BEING A FAILURE IS IMAPRTIVE AS IF TODAY YOU ARE A FAILURE BUT THEN TOMORROW YOU WILL BE A SUCCESSFUL PERSON,TODAY EVERYONE WILL TEASE YOU BECAUSE YOU ARE A FAILURE BUT TOMORROW EVERYONE WILL OBEY YOU FOR BEING A SUCCESSFUL PERSON.THIS WORLD IS FULL OF DIFFICULT THINGS BUT NOTHING IS IMPOSSIBLE IN THIS WORLD. ALWAYS BELIVE IN THE IMPOSSIBLE.

SIX

CHAPTER6:WHY FAILURE IS THE BEST TEACHER??

AS TRULY SAID "FAILURE IS THE BEST TEACHER" BECAUSE FAILURE MAKES YOU RE-THINK,CREATIVE AND ETC.SUCCESS IS GOOD BUT FAILURE IS BEETER.LIFE IS A MIXTURE OF SUCCESS AND FAIIURE.FAILURES ARE THE PILLARS OF SUCCESS.FAILURE NEVER FALLS YOU BUT IT GROWS YOU.FAILURE MAKE YOU A TREE FROM A SMALL PLANT.SUCCESS IS A HILL BUT FAILURE IS A MOUNTAIN.

SEVEN

WHY FAILURE LEADS TO SUCCESS??

IT HELPS IN GAINING KNOWLEDGE.FAILURE SHOW YOU THE WAY TO SUCCESS.FAILURE DOESNT MEAN YOU ARE A FAILURE BUT FAILURE MEANS THAT YOU HAVENT SUCCEED YET.FAILURE DOESNT MEAN THAT YOU ARE A LOSER BUT FAILURE MEANS YOU A WINNER.FAILURE BRINGS THE OPPORTUNITY TO LEARN THINGS BETTER.ACCORDING TO MICHEAL JORDAN "I HAVE LOST ALMOST 300 GAMES.26 TIMES I HAVE BEEN TRUSTED TO TAKE THE GAME WINNING SHOT AND I HAVE MISSED.I HAVE FAILED OVER AND OVER AGAIN IN MY LIFE AND THAT IS WHY I SUCCEED"FAILURE IS THE FUEL FOR SUCCESS.WORST MAKES YOU THE BEST.

THANK YOU FOR READING MY BOOK HPE YOU LIKED THIS BOOK.